Solder Anythin

Charms Shown
Actual Size

Basic Soldering Techniques

A. Collage or find an image to fit the shape of the glass.

B. Sandwich images between two pieces of glass.

Tip: Decorate both sides.

You can turn any small object into a pendant by soldering around it and attaching a jump ring. In these samples, coins and amusement park tokens, game pieces, vintage pictures, bits of glass, ceramic tile, and plastic have all been used to create art.

1. Clean the glass with alcohol or glass cleaner using a cotton swab.

2. Peel off Copper tape backing a small amount at a time. Wrap the glass edges,

centering the glass in the middle of the tape. Work your way around all the sides, letting the tape overlap about 1/4". Remove excess with scissors.

3. Miter the corners. Using fine detail scissors, snip a small "V" shape in each of the corners so tape will lay flat against glass.

4. Burnish well using a bone folder. The heat from the soldering iron can curl poorly burnished tape away from the glass.

5. Start with the glass piece laying flat on a heat resistant surface. Apply flux using a cotton swab around the edges.

6. Unroll a bit of solder. Hold the tip of the iron against the edge of the solder. Wait for it

to start to melt and form a small bead of solder at the end of the tip. Apply a bead of solder to the edge of the glass piece. In a smooth motion, drag the bead across the surface.

Continued on page 4

Solder Anything!

Continued from page 3

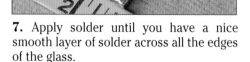

7. Apply solder until you have a nice smooth layer of solder across all the edges of the glass.

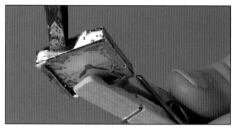

8. Flip the glass piece over. Flux and solder the other side. Then, flux and solder the edges.

9. Flux and add solder to anchor the jump ring to the top.

10. Clean with a flux remover and warm water. Then use solder polish for extra shine.

Great Tips:

- *Drag the tip of the iron across a wet sponge when dark spots start appearing. When the solder gets difficult to melt, try cleaning the tip of the iron with sal ammoniac.*

- *If the solder appears too thin, try applying another layer.*

- *Peeling off the entire backing of the Copper tape at once makes it difficult to work with because it twists and curls. Remove only a small bit of the backing at a time.*

- *Dab the edge of your flux-saturated cotton swab off before applying to the Copper tape. Too much flux can cause gritty solder and oxidation.*

Black and Copper Patina Framed Charms

Safety Precautions -

Soldering is fun and simple, but always remember that you are working with hazardous materials. To prevent burns, remove all metal jewelry before soldering. If jewelry removal is not possible, cover exposed metal with masking tape. • Pay attention to your surroundings at all times. If you smell something burning, quickly check out the situation. Keep the iron in its stand when not in use. Keep the tip away from anything that is flammable or can melt. • Wear safety goggles and a mask at all times. The fumes from flux, solder, patinas and sal ammoniac can be hazardous. Work outdoors or in a well-ventilated space.

Soldering Iron

Rheostat

Glass

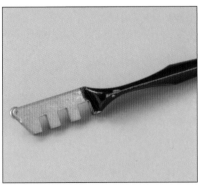

Glass cutter

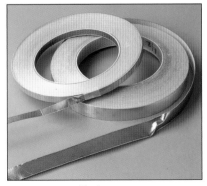

Foil tape

Tools and Equipment

Having the right tools will make the job easier and more professional looking.

Here is an explanation of the tools used in soldering.

Soldering Iron - Used to melt solder onto metal surface. For jewelry and craft soldering, use a 75-100 watt iron with a Rheostat and a stand. Butane torch irons are also available.

Rheostat - Temperature control gauge for the soldering iron. Using the correct temperature prolongs the life of your tip and controls the flow of the solder. Too much heat can melt the foil tape and can cause solder to drip off the tip. If the setting is too cold, the solder will not melt. When you first turn on your iron, turn the control to its highest setting, wait 3-5 minutes, then turn it down to about mid-way.
 **Temperatures are given in °F.

Glass - You can use anything from clear to colored to hand-made glass for soldered art. Some handle the heat better than others. Slide glass is easy to cut, is lightweight, but is thin and has sharp edges. Glass from a stained glass supplier is durable.

Cutting Glass - Glass cutting takes quite a bit of practice to perfect. It's easier to buy precut glass. If you are determined to cut your own glass, practice on scrap glass until you are comfortable doing it.

Glass Cutting Tool - Used to make a score line in the glass. For best results, hold the tool so the blade is vertical. Using the right pressure (you will hear a slight cutting noise, not a horrible grating sound), move the tool in a smooth, straight line across the glass. Pausing or trying to score the same line twice will make jagged edges. Depending on the thickness of the glass, you can either snap the glass apart, or use breaking pliers to cut the glass. *Burnt Offerings* makes a glass cutting jig that makes cutting slide glass a breeze.

Foil Tape - Copper foil tape is the surface upon which you solder. It comes in widths from 1/8" to 1/2". The choice of width is determined by the thickness of the glass you use. Silvered Copper tape is available and although more expensive than regular copper tape, it is good for beginners because you don't have to cover all the visible Copper.

Sal Ammoniac Block - Used for keeping the tip of your iron clean and tinned, therefore making the flow of solder easier and faster. Follow the manufacturer's directions carefully. Use only as necessary and avoid breathing the fumes.

Flux - Used to adhere solder to the Copper tape. Leftover flux can corrode the solder and leave it appearing dull, so clean your soldered piece well with a flux remover and warm water after you are finished.

Solder - We used lead-free solder because lead causes cancer and other serious health problems. For decorative soldering, lead-free solder works wonderfully. However, it melts at a higher temperature than lead solder, so you need to replace your soldering tip more often. Take extra care in cleaning and caring for your iron to extend the longevity of your tool.

Patinas - Patinas change the color of your solder, which is normally Silver in color. Color options include Black and Copper.

Soldering Jig - Useful in adding jump rings to soldered pieces. Can also be used to correctly align soldered pieces to form a chain link. Made from a heat-resistant material that makes it ideal for soldering on top of.

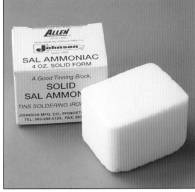

Sal Ammoniac

Flux

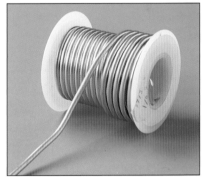

Lead-free solder

Patina

Soldering Jig

Soldered Pins

by Carrie Edelmann-Avery

Combine vintage photos, collage art and rubber stamping to create your own line of designer jewelry. Soldering allows you to personalize each piece. When you give these unique gifts, everyone will want to know where you bought it. You will be so proud to say, "I made it myself!"

GENERAL MATERIALS:
16-18 gauge metal sheet • Jump rings • Pin back • Tin snips • Bone folder • Solder supplies (solder, iron, flux, flux cleaner, polish, jig, 1/4" Copper tape) • Epoxy glue

GENERAL INSTRUCTIONS:
Stamp and collage images as needed. Cut images to fit glass. Trace glass shapes onto metal sheet. Use tin snips to cut the metal sheet to size. Layer the image between the glass and metal. • Wrap Copper tape around all edges. Miter corners and burnish well with a bone folder. Flux and solder over the Copper tape. Using the jig, align the jump rings against the ruler on the jig. Flux the jump rings and add solder to anchor. • Join 2 soldered pieces together using jump rings.

Glue a pin back to the top soldered piece. Place a small piece of Copper tape over the pin back. Flux and solder over the Copper tape. Clean well with flux remover and warm water. Polish if desired.

Granny's Cart
MATERIALS: Rectangle shaped glass • Vintage photo • *American Traditional* bird rub-on

Always Friends
MATERIALS: Rectangle shaped glass • *Eclectic Omnibus* friends image • *Pebbles, Inc.* decorative paper

Desire
MATERIALS: Shaped glass (house, rectangle) • *Eclectic Omnibus* face image • *FoofaLa* words • *Pebbles, Inc.* heart image

Mermaid
MATERIALS: Shaped glass (house, rectangle) • *Bearing Beads* mermaid clip art • *FoofaLa* words • *Acey Deucy* shell rubber stamp • *Clearsnap* Ancient Page Coal Black ink pad

1. Cut image to fit glass.

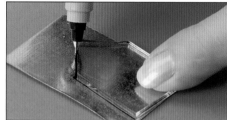

2. Trace the glass shape onto the metal sheet.

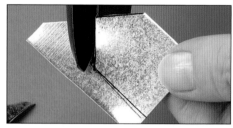

3. Cut out metal shape.

4. Layer metal, image and glass.

5. Wrap with foil tape.

6. Solder over foil tape.

7. Completely cover tape with solder.

8. Use the jig to position jump rings.

9. Solder jump rings in place.

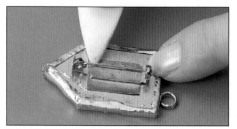

10. Place copper over pin back, burnish well, then flux and solder.

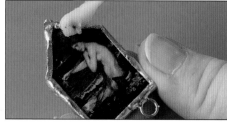

11. Clean piece with cotton swab.

12. Attach pieces with jump rings.

1. Stamp image on glass.

2. Solder edges.

3. Place piece on jig.

4. Solder jump rings.

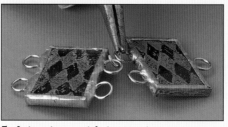

5. Join piece with jump rings.

6. Solder jump rings closed.

Bracelets
Creative Designs

Lasso the best bracelet for yourself or that special "cowgirl-wanna-be". Silver, glass and beads round-up an opulent look. The letter blocks have images of wild west cowgirls on the back.

Express your artistic talent in a stunning stained glass wearable. These bracelets are so beautiful you will want to make all of them.

Cowgirl Jump Ring Bracelet

by Carrie Edelmann-Avery

MATERIALS: 14 pieces of $5/8$" x $3/4$" cut glass • *Bearing Beads* cowgirl images • *Pebbles, Inc.* Alphabet letters • Chain • Toggle clasp • Jump rings • Beads • Head pins • Pliers (needle-nose, chain-nose) • Solder supplies (solder, iron, flux, flux remover, polish, jig, $3/8$" Copper tape)

INSTRUCTIONS: **Charms:** Cut images and layer between glass. • Wrap each set of glass pieces with Copper tape. Miter corners and burnish well. • **Solder:** Flux and solder over Copper tape. Using jig, solder jump rings to the top of each piece. Clean and polish each piece. • **Assembly:** Lay out chain and place pieces to determine placement. Attach soldered charms to the chain with jump rings. • **Beaded dangles:** Add beads to head pins leaving at least half of the pin without beads. Starting $1/4$" from the last bead, bend the head pin around needle-nose pliers to form a loop. Slide the dangle on the chain, bend the rest of the wire around the head pin until fully wrapped. • **Clasp:** Add toggle clasp to the end of the chain with jump rings.

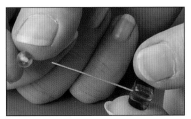
1. Add beads to head pin.

2. Bend the wire into a loop.

3. Attach to bracelet.

Reverse Stained Glass Bracelet

by Beckah Krahula

MATERIALS: 5 equal charm-sized glass pieces • Rubber stamps (*Bearing Beads, JudiKins, Clearsnap*) • *Ranger* Cut n' Dry foam stamp pad • Jump rings • Clasp • Bone folder • 91% Rubbing Alcohol • Cotton swabs • Needle-nose pliers • Wooden clothespins • *Pebeo* Vitrea (160 Diluents; 160 Brilliant or Frost Medium) • *Houston Art* (Authentic Metal Powders, Gloss Medium, Sealer) • Push pins • Solder supplies (solder, iron, flux, jig, $1/4$" Copper tape)

INSTRUCTIONS: Clean glass with alcohol and swabs. • Mix 2 parts Gloss or Frost Medium to 1 part Diluent to 1 part Metal Powders. • Test a stamp on parchment. If the image is too transparent, add powder. If it won't stamp, add more medium. Create 1-2 inks for the front and back of the glass charms. Use Gloss for a leaf finish and Frost for a raw metal finish. Apply metallic ink to the stamp pad foam. Stamp all the charm backs. Let dry. Remix the ink for the top of the charms. Apply ink to stamp pad foam. Stamp the front of all the pieces and allow to dry. • Place charms on an Aluminum foil covered cookie sheet and put on the center rack of a cold oven. Bring oven to 275°. Cure for 30 minutes. Shut off the oven, open the door, and allow the charms to cool gradually in the oven. • Wrap the edges of each piece of glass with Copper tape. Miter the corners, and burnish well. Flux and solder all 4 edges. • Use push pins in the predrilled holes to secure one charm between 2 balsa strips of the jig. This charm will have 3 jump rings soldered to it: one on the right $1/2$" down and two $1/4$" from the top and bottom on the left. Use the measuring tape on the jig to line these up. • Close the split in the jump rings. Apply solder to jump ring and the charm where the ring will attach. Use a small screwdriver or a pair of needle-nose pliers to hold ring in place on jig. Pick up the solder on the end of the iron and apply to fluxed area. • All the center charms get jump rings soldered 2 on each side, $1/4$" from the top and bottom. The last charm gets the jump rings soldered 2 on the left, $1/4$" from top and bottom and 1 on the right, $1/2$" down. • Use jump rings to string charms together and apply clasps. • Solder the jump rings closed. • Wash bracelet, seal and polish if desired.

Pendant Necklaces

These charming pendants with their house shape invoke all the emotions of home. Each piece has a door masked off so a tiny image shows through. Because the piece is made from two glass shapes, the pendant is reversible.

Wearable Domestic Shrine Necklace
by Beckah Krahula

MATERIALS: *Bearing Beads* (2 house-shaped 1" x 1 3/4" glass pieces, Transfer sheets, Soldering jig) • *Teesha Moore* Metal Leaf rubber stamp • Jump rings • 91% Rubbing alcohol • Cotton swabs • Needle-nose pliers • *DesignaSize* Quick Pen Gold Leaf adhesive • Scissors • Bone folder • Chamois piece • 1/2" Foam brush • Lint-free towel • *Pebeo* Vitrea (160 Diluent, 160 Brilliant or Frost Medium) • *Houston Art* (Imitation Silver Leaf, Authentic Metal Powders, Gloss Medium, Sealer, Omni-Gel) • Solder supplies (solder, iron, flux, Copper patina)

INSTRUCTIONS: Clean glass. **First glass**: Mix 2 parts Gloss or Frost Medium to 1 part Diluent to 1 part Authentic Metal Powders. Test on parchment. If image is too transparent, add powder. If it won't stamp, add more medium. • Create 1-2 inks, for the front and back of the glass charm. Use Gloss for a leaf finish and Frost for a raw metal finish. • Mask off a 1/2" x 5/8" door. • Apply metallic ink for the background stamp to the stamp pad foam. Stamp image. Let dry completely. Place charm on an Aluminum foil covered cookie sheet and put on the center rack of a cold oven. Bring oven to 275°. Cure for 30 minutes. Shut off oven, open door, and allow charms to cool gradually in the oven. • **Second glass**: Prepare transfer sheets with 3 coats of Omni-Gel following manufacturer's instructions. Let dry. • Cut out image that will be transferred to the glass. Heat set the image using a 225° tack iron. Tack for 30 seconds, then iron from the center out for 30 seconds. Remember to get the edges. Let cool. Soak in warm water for 1-2 minutes and roll paper off the back of the transfer. Clean lint off with a damp lint-free towel, working over the piece in circular motions. Let dry. • Paint the glass the transfer is on with the sizing pen. Let dry completely. • Place colored foil in the areas you like. Brush off excess. • **Assembly**: Place the front and back houses together with the metal stamping on the outside. • Wrap the edges of the glass with Copper tape. Burnish well. Flux and solder over the Copper tape. Add flux to jump ring and solder on top of the pendant. • Wash piece and polish.

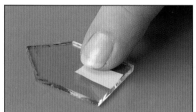
1. Mask off door area.

2. Prepare the transfer with Omni-Gel.

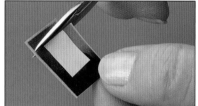
3. Cut out image for door.

4. Heat image on glass.

5. Roll paper off image.

6. Clean glass.

1. Transfer image to glass.

2. Apply leaf sizing.

3. Apply gold leaf to the back of the image.

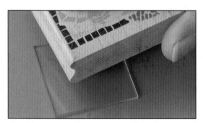
4. Stamp the second piece of glass.

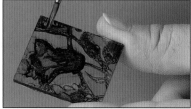
5. Paint glass with alcohol ink.

6. Place the glass pieces back to back.

Wear a stained glass art piece or show off a vintage tin image on a reversible necklace. This technique uses two pieces of glass decorated separately to make this effect.

Reversible Necklaces

Faux Tin Type Necklace   *by Beckah Krahula*

MATERIALS: *Bearing Beads* (2 pieces 1¼" x 1½" glass; Transfer sheets) • *Postmodern Design* rubber stamps • Jump rings • Necklace chain • *Ranger* Alcohol inks • Scissors • Bone folder • Chamois piece • 91% Rubbing alcohol • Cotton swabs • Needle-nose pliers • *DesignaSize* Quick Pen Gold Leaf adhesive • ½" Foam brush • *Houston Art* (Omni-Gel, Imitation Silver Leaf, Authentic Metal Powders, Gloss Medium, Sealer) • *Pebeo* Vitrea (160 Diluents, 160 Brilliant or Frost medium) • Solder supplies (solder, iron, flux, jig, 5/16" scalloped Copper tape)

INSTRUCTIONS: Prepare transfer sheets with 3 coats of Omni-Gel, following manufacturer's instructions. Clean both pieces of glass with rubbing alcohol. • **First piece of glass**: Once Omni-Gel is dry, cut out image that will be transferred to the glass. Heat set the image to the smooth side of the glass using a 225° tack iron. Tack for 30 seconds, then iron from the center out for 30 seconds. Remember to get the edges. Let cool. Soak in warm water for 1-2 minutes and roll paper off the back of the transfer. Clean lint off with a damp lint-free chamois working over the piece in circular motions. Set aside to dry. Use the Quick Pen to apply sizing/gold leaf adhesive to the back of the transferred charm. Set aside to dry. • Apply Silver leaf and set aside. • **Second piece of glass**: Mix 2 parts Gloss or Frost Medium to 1 part Diluent to 1 part Authentic Metal Powders. Test on parchment. If image is too transparent, add powder. If it won't stamp, add more medium. Use Gloss for a leaf finish and Frost for a raw metal finish. • Apply metallic ink for the background stamp to the stamp pad foam. Stamp image and let dry completely. • Paint the back of this piece of glass with Alcohol Inks. Let dry completely. • **Assembly**: Put ink side of the second piece of glass against the leaf side of the first. Wrap all of the edges of the glass with Copper tape. Use the bone folder to burnish edges on charm. Then turn the edges of the tape over onto the top of the charm, miter corners, and burnish. Repeat on back. • Flux and solder over the Copper tape. Add flux to jump ring and solder to the top of the pendant. • Clean piece and polish if desired.

Doll Pendants

by Linda and Opie O'Brien

Pendants are more fun when they have many pieces. These doll and wire frame pendants have dangling parts. The movement catches the eye. Make your piece personal with images and words that are meaningful to you.

Broken Heart Doll Pendant
MATERIALS: Oil pencils • Black permanent ink • Text • Limb charms
INSTRUCTIONS: See Doll Pendant Instructions.

Mona Lisa Doll Pendant
MATERIALS: Shoe charms
INSTRUCTIONS: See Doll Pendant Instructions.

Doll Pendant
GENERAL MATERIALS: Glass slides • *Burnt Offerings* (clip art, rubber stamp) • Glass cutter • Glass cutting jig • 18 gauge tinned Copper wire • Pliers (round-nose, flat-nose) • Wire cutters • Solder supplies (solder, iron, flux, 1/4" Copper tape) • Glue stick
INSTRUCTIONS: Use the glass cutting jig and template to cut slides into desired shapes. Cut images to the size of glass. Sandwich images between glass slides. • Wrap with Copper tape. Miter corners and burnish well. Flux and solder over the Copper tape. Clean with flux remover. To join the slides and/or add beads or charms, creatively bend and twist the wire around the slide. Flux and solder where the wire touches the solder.

Wire Wrap Pendants

by Ramona Dolan Ashman and Tom Ashman

This technique uses wire wrapping to emphasize the slide image and provides an alternative to soldering a jump ring or attaching a clasp to the slide for chain attachment. The solder in this example is layered to add texture.

Adding an additional layer of glass gives depth to the image, increases the weight of the piece, and also gives it the feel of real jewelry.

Madame Butterfly Pendant
MATERIALS: 3 microscope slides • 6 images for collage • *ARTchix Studio* transparency • Jewelry chain • *Triangle Coatings* (Sophisticated Finishes Primer, Sealer) • Chain-nose pliers • Flush wire cutters • 16-18 gauge tinned Copper wire • Solder supplies (solder, iron, flux, Copper tape)
INSTRUCTIONS: Follow General Instructions for Wire Wrapping.

Fairest of Them All Pendant
MATERIALS: 3 microscope slides • *ARTchix Studio* images • Transparency printed by inkjet printer • Chain-nose pliers • 16-18 gauge tinned Copper wire • Solder supplies (solder, iron, flux, Copper tape)
INSTRUCTIONS: Place the top image and the bottom image back to back on top of the first slide. Cover with second slide. Add transparency to the top of the second slide. Follow General Instructions for Wire Wrapping.

Create a Message

Create your own message or remind yourself to "create" great art with this fun and easy wire wrapping project. Use chain and needle-nose pliers to bend wire into interesting shapes and patterns. Solder a few points on the wire to make sure it stays in place on the slides.

Create
by Carrie Edelmann-Avery

MATERIALS: *Design Originals* #0616 Walnut Water Spots paper • 12 pieces slide glass • *Making Memories* alphabet stamps • *Ranger* Black Soot Distress Inks • 16-20 gauge Sterling Silver wire • Pliers (needle-nose, chain-nose) • Wire cutters • Solder supplies (solder, iron, flux, flux remover, polish, 1/4" Copper tape)
INSTRUCTIONS: Follow General Instructions for Wire Wrapping.

Wire Wrapping
by Ramona Dolan Ashman and Tom Ashman

GENERAL INSTRUCTIONS: Layer images between the microscope slides. • Apply Copper tape to the edges of the glass. Miter the corners, and burnish the sides down. Apply flux and solder over the tape. Allow the slide to cool. • Turn down the temperature of the iron until the solder just barely melts when warmed by the iron. Layer a thick seam of solder over the edges of the piece. While the solder is cooling, lightly tap it again with the warm, but not hot, iron. This creates the peaks in the thick solder border. When finished, clean the piece and polish. • Cut 12" of tinned Copper wire. Begin at the top of the slide by creating a curl, loop or spiral with chain-nose pliers. Then wrap the wire around the slide, spiraling downward until you reach the bottom corner. At the bottom corner loop the wire once to "catch" the corner and secure the slide from slipping. Freehand loop and spiral the remainder of the wire. Add a small curl to hang a charm at the end if you wish. Seal with primer and clear sealer. • Add jewelry chain or wire hanger.

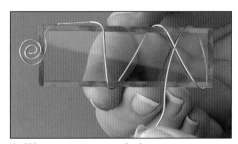

1. Wrap wire around glass.

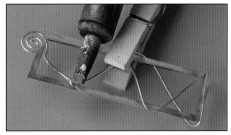

2. Solder wire to glass.

Gourd Tokens

by Linda Rael

These unique pieces have a wonderful texture and light weight. Made from gourds, these projects are very natural and rustic looking.

Framed Portrait Brooch

MATERIALS: Gourd shape • Clip art • Square frame • Pin back • *Jacquard* Pinata inks • Scissors • Bone folder • Acrylic nail sanding block • Scalloped Copper tape • Solder supplies (solder, iron, flux, Copper tape, Black Patina) • *JudiKins* Diamond Glaze

INSTRUCTIONS: Cut square shape from gourd shell. Sand well. • Add a square frame in the center with Copper tape. Adhere scalloped Copper tape around gourd edges, smooth with bone folder. • Flux, solder, and patina over the Copper tape. • Lightly sand over solder with acrylic nail sanding block. • Adhere and seal photo with Diamond Glaze. • Paint the back of the brooch with Pinata ink. Smudge a small amount of ink on the front of the gourd shell. Glue on pin back.

Inspire Bracelet

MATERIALS: Gourd pieces • Copper jump rings • Rubber stamps • *Making Memories* triangle jump rings • *Rings & Things* Purchased chain bracelet • Scissors • Bone folder • Sandpaper • *Golden* Matte Gel medium • Solder supplies (solder, iron, flux, Copper tape, Black Patina)

INSTRUCTIONS: Cut 7 round shapes from gourd shell and sand all sides. Edge rounds with Copper tape. Flux and solder over Copper tape. Solder Copper jump rings. Patina using Black solution. Lightly sand surface of solder when dry. • Stamp letters and spirals on old paper, tear out to fit onto gourd pieces. Adhere and seal with Matte Medium. Letters on front spell "INSPIRE". Spirals are stamped on the back. • Use triangle jump rings to attach charms to bracelet.

Moon Joy

MATERIALS: Gourd shape • "Joy" stamp • Scrap of paper • Pin back • Scalloped Copper tape • Moon shaped bone piece • Acrylic nail block • Scissors • Bone folder • *Golden* Matte Gel medium • Sandpaper • Solder supplies (solder, iron, flux, Black Patina, Copper tape) • *JudiKins* Diamond Glaze

INSTRUCTIONS: Cut square from gourd shell. Sand well. • Edge gourd piece with scalloped Copper tape. Edge bone moon with scalloped Copper tape. Smooth with bone folder. • Flux, solder, and patina over the Copper tape. Sand with acrylic nail block. • Stamp "Joy" on old paper. Glue and coat paper and gourd shell with Matte Gel Medium. Glue on moon face with Diamond Glaze. Glue on pin back.

Flower Brooch

MATERIALS: Gourd shape • Pin back • Water-based sealer • Scissors • Bone folder • Sandpaper • Solder supplies (solder, iron, flux, Copper tape, Black Patina) • Black pearls • Adhesive

INSTRUCTIONS: Cut and sand gourd. • Add Copper tape around edge and in center in flower shape. Smooth with bone folder. • Flux, solder, and patina over the Copper tape. Patina a decorative brad collar with Black solution. Glue in flower center. Glue on Black pearls and pin back. Brush on water-based sealer on front and back of the exposed gourd.

Leaf Pendant

MATERIALS: Gourd shape • Scalloped Copper tape • Leather cord • *Jacquard* Pinata ink • Scissors • Bone folder • Drill • Sandpaper • Solder supplies (solder, iron, flux, Copper tape, Black Patina) • 4 Head pins • 4 Crystal beads • Glue

INSTRUCTIONS: Cut a leaf shape from dried, hard-shelled gourd. Sand well. • Add Copper tape on all edges. Smooth with bone folder. Add scalloped Copper tape (double tape lines with straight sides back to back) to make a double scalloped leaf vein pattern. Add more tape across the stem area. Flux, solder, and patina over the Copper tape. • Dab Pinata inks in Greens and Reds on the surface of the gourd between soldered lines. • Drill holes at stem end and on leaf. Glue head pins and tiny crystal beads into holes. Add cord through stem hole.

Bottle Cap Tokens

by Laura Dehart

The bottle caps in this set are all decorated using the same technique. The variations occur when the bottle caps are soldered together.

Change the look of each piece by flattening the flange with a mallet, or leave alone for a deeper frame. Experiment with different materials - stickers, photos, seashells, buttons, marbles and game pieces - for your caps.

Bottle Cap Bracelet

GENERAL MATERIALS: *Design Originals* (11 Bottle Caps; Papers: #0579 ABCs Dictionary, #0580 School Books, #0597 Fortune Cards, #0600 Dominoes) • Vellum • Jump rings • Scissors • Pencil • Flat-nose pliers • Sandpaper • *Rings N Things* (Curb chain bracelet, Bracelet form, Lobster claw clasp) • *Krylon* fixative • *JudiKins* Diamond Glaze • Solder supplies (solder, iron, flux) • Optional (acrylic paint, paintbrush)

BOTTLE CAP INSTRUCTIONS: **Images**: Make a vellum template to fit inside the bottle cap. Trace and cut out chosen images. Place images inside the bottle cap. Fold over the bottle cap pleats with flat-nose pliers to secure the image inside.

Soldered Bottle Cap Bracelet Form

INSTRUCTIONS: Follow Bottle Cap Instructions. • **Prep**: Lightly sand the backs of the bottle caps. Turn the bottle caps sanded side up and lay the bracelet form circles over the bottle caps. • **Soldering**: Flux and solder every other bracelet form circle to the bottle caps. • **Images**: To apply a glaze to the image inside the bottle caps, spray workable fixative according to the manufacturer's instructions. (The fixative keeps the ink from running when you apply the Diamond Glaze.) Let Dry. • Squeeze enough Diamond Glaze to cover the image. Let dry overnight.

Jump Ring Link Bracelet

INSTRUCTIONS: Follow Bottle Cap Instructions. • **Jump rings**: Flux and solder jump rings perpendicular to the top of the bottle cap. • Add a second jump ring, soldering it parallel with the top of the bottle cap. Loop the jump rings around one another and close with flat-nose pliers. • **Clasp**: Attach a lobster claw clasp with a jump ring and close with flat-nose pliers. Solder the jump rings closed for permanency.

Tips:

Sand all the finish off the area to be soldered. • To solder jump rings, use a soldering jig. Lay the bottle cap image side up on the soldering jig.

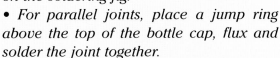

• For parallel joints, place a jump ring above the top of the bottle cap, flux and solder the joint together.

• For perpendicular joints, hold the jump ring against the top of the bottle cap with flat-nosed pliers. Flux and solder the joint.

Multi Color Bracelet

INSTRUCTIONS: Follow Bottle Cap Instructions. • **Jump rings**: Flux and solder jump rings perpendicular to the top of the bottle cap. Loop the jump rings around the bracelet and close with flat-nose pliers. • **Clasp**: Attach a lobster claw clasp with a jump ring and close with flat-nose pliers. Solder the jump rings closed for permanency. • **Decorations**: Paint the edges of the bottle caps with assorted colors of acrylic if desired.

Matching Earrings and Pendant

INSTRUCTIONS: Follow Bottle Cap Instructions, inserting foreign coins instead of paper images. • **Jump rings**: Flux and solder jump rings to the top of the bottle cap. Loop the jump rings through the earring finding or pendant jump ring.

Cositas

by Beckah Krahula and Carrie Edelmann-Avery

1. Wrap shapes with copper tape.

2. Position shape on jig.

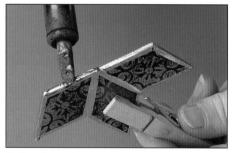

3. Solder edges.

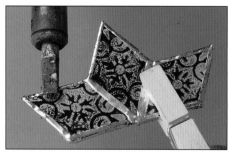

4. Build up decorative edge of solder.

5. Repeat soldering on the back.

Cositas in Spanish means "pretty little things". It's a fitting description for these wonderful projects with a stained glass look.

Brilliant vitrea will produce a metal look, while frost gives an oxidized look. The red diamonds were stamped with frost, while the yellow diamonds were stamped with Brilliant.

Choose the design medium that best suits the project you are creating.

Cositas

MATERIALS: Two 2¹/2" x 3" clear pieces of glass • Six 1" diamond shaped glass pieces • 3" images for transfer • *Pebeo* (Vitrea :160 Diluents, 160 Brilliant or Frost; Glass markers) • *Houston Art* (Omni-Gel, Authentic Metal Powders) • *Ranger* 2¹/2" x 3" Cut n' Dry stamp pad • *Postmodern Design* rubber stamps • Parchment paper • Bone folder • Push pins • 1" foam brush • Scissors • Craft knife • Lint-free cloth • Leafing Adhesive Pen • Silver leaf • Alcohol inks (*Jacquard* Piñata or *Ranger*) • Clothespin • Solder supplies (solder, iron, flux, jig, patina)

INSTRUCTIONS: **First rectangle**: Clean glass. Follow the manufacturer's instructions for Omni-Gel to transfer the image to the first piece of 2¹/2" x 3" glass. Let dry. Place a coat of leaf adhesive on the other side of the glass. Set aside to dry. Place Silver leaf over dried adhesive and brush away excess.

• **Stamping**: The 6 diamond shapes and 1 of the large rectangles are stamped with metallic inks. • In a disposable cup, use a popsicle stick to mix 2 parts Pebeo Gloss or Frost Medium to 1 part Pebeo Diluent to 2 parts Authentic Metal Powders. Test on parchment. If image is too transparent, add powder. If it won't stamp, add more medium. • Apply metallic ink to the Cut n' Dry pad, and ink the stamp. Stamp image onto the back of the second rectangles. • Stamp all the backs of each diamond. Allow to dry for a couple minutes. • Stamp the front of all the pieces and allow to dry. • Place diamonds and rectangle on an aluminum foil covered cookie sheet and put into the center rack of a cold oven. Bring oven to 275°. Set timer and cure for 30 minutes. The cure time starts when the oven reaches 275°. Shut off oven. Open door, and allow pieces to cool gradually in the oven.

• **Prep**: Place the stamped rectangle over the Silver leaf side of the transferred rectangle and wrap the 2 together with Copper tape. Burnish and set aside. • Wrap all diamonds with Copper tape and burnish the edges with a bone folder. Overlap the end of the Copper tape by ¹/2" to strengthen the soldering. Pin the top 3 diamonds together on the jig and flux the front edge of all 3 diamonds.

• **Soldering**: Pick up a bead of solder on the iron and run it along the fluxed Copper like a pencil. Let cool. Go back over the diamonds again, building up a rounded layer of solder. Flip over and repeat for the back. Set aside. • Repeat the previous step for the other set of diamonds.

• **Assembly**: Pin the top set of diamonds onto the jig and align the top of the glass rectangle with the bottom of the diamonds. Use more push pins to hold in place. Flux and solder the diamond top to the rectangle. Let cool. • Repeat on the back. Let cool. • Repeat the previous step to solder the bottom set of diamonds onto the bottom of the glass rectangle. • Place the Cositas in a clothespin. Solder the edges. • Solder the hanger to the back of the Cositas. Let cool.

• **Decorative Finish**: Come back with the broad area of your soldering iron and bead across the solder on the front to add a decorative finish to the solder. Wash piece. Rinse and dry. • Brush patina onto solder if desired.

Untraditional Frames

by Carrie Edelmann-Avery

This 1940's vintage shot was taken in a photo booth. This frame variation uses solder to completely cover the copper tape. To give the frame the nostalgic look that complements the photo, black patina was applied over the solder.

Vintage Photo Booth

MATERIALS: 2 pieces $2^3/4$" x 4" clear glass • $3^1/2$" ball chain • Photograph • Solder supplies (solder, iron, flux, flux remover, $1/2$" Copper tape, Black patina) • Double-sided tape

INSTRUCTIONS: Follow instructions for Clear Hanging Frames. Continue soldering until all Copper tape is completely covered. • Clean solder. • Apply Black patina to age solder.

Clear Hanging Frames

WEDDING MATERIALS: $1/2$" Copper tape • 10" large ball chain • 2 pieces $5^1/2$" x $7^3/4$" handmade crackle glass • Photograph • Solder supplies (solder, iron, flux, Copper patina) • Double-sided tape

GRAND CANYON MATERIALS: 10" large ball chain • 2 pieces $5^1/2$" x $8^1/2$" glass • Photograph • Solder supplies (solder, iron, flux, $1/2$" Copper tape, Copper patina) • Double-sided tape

INSTRUCTIONS: Clean glass. Apply a small amount of double-sided tape to the back of the photo. Center and adhere photo to 1 piece of glass. Cover the photo with the other piece of glass. • Wrap the edges of the glass with Copper tape. Miter the corners and burnish well. • Cut a 1" length of $1/2$" Copper tape. Cover one end of the ball chain with the tape and adhere to the edge of the top of the glass. Repeat on the other side. • Flux and solder over the tape on the ball chain. Apply Copper Patina to the solder to match the tape.

continued on pages 20 - 21

1. Adhere photo to clean glass.

2. Sandwich the photo between the glass pieces.

3. Cover one end of the ball chain with copper tape. Repeat on other end.

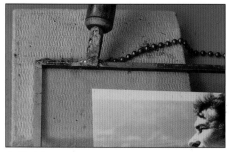

4. Solder over copper tape.

5. Apply patina with a brush.

Instead of the usual mat, clear glass surrounds this wedding photo and this memory of the Grand Canyon, creating a light airy feeling and emphasizing the photo as focal point. Save this technique for your most eye-catching pictures.

Frames

Continued from pages 18 - 19

These two frames illustrate one of the best reasons you will want to learn to solder - you can make a beautiful frame in any size you want!

If you have a wonderful photo in an odd shape, you can craft a special frame for it.

There's nothing like being able to say "I did it myself."

Now you can wear your favorite flowers, perfectly preserved, forever.

These pendants are a natural for gift giving and wearing every day. Use the flowers from your garden to make your pendant truly personal, or purchase a pressed tropical for a more exotic creation. Everyone will love this beautiful collection from nature.

Diva Doll

by Carrie Edelmann-Avery

This doll reminds you to follow your inner vision and "live happy". Assorted beads become pretty arms, and the clip art face is easily replaced by a photo of a loved one.

This project would look lovely hanging in a window.

MATERIALS: *Design Originals* (1 Bottle Cap; Papers: #0526 Two Ladies, #0528 Watches) • *Bearing Beads* (Soldering Jig, clip art) • *Burnt Offering* Glass Cutting Jig • Glass slides (Four 1" x 3", Four 1" x 2¹/4") • *Making Memories* Rub-On word "vision" • Beads • Hand charms • *Poetry Dog Tags* Chronicle Books • Jump rings • Purchased necklace chain • Wire • Eye pins • Pliers (needle-nose, flat-nose) • Wire cutters • Scissors • Bone folder • *Golden* Matte Medium • Solder supplies (solder, flux, iron, ¹/4" Silvered Copper tape) • *JudiKins* Diamond Glaze • 1" hole punch

INSTRUCTIONS: Punch clip art face to fit inside bottle cap. Adhere and cover with Matte Medium. Let dry. • Cut Two Ladies paper to fit 1" x 2¹/4" top slide. Write "inner" and rub on "vision". • Cut clip art guitar for 1" x 2¹/4" second slide. Cut Watches paper for 1" x 3" "leg" slides. • Wrap edges of all the slides with Copper tape. Flux and solder over the Copper tape. • Align slide pieces to determine placement of jump rings. Using soldering jig, place each slide onto jig and solder jump rings into place. Clean slide pieces with flux remover. Attach slide pieces together with jump rings. • Thread beads onto eye pin to form arms. Wrap the end of the eye pin through the hand charm, and attach the other end to the jump rings at the shoulders. Curl a piece of wire into a figure 8 shape and adhere to the back of the bottle cap. Attach bottle cap face to the body with a jump ring. Attach metal dog tag feet with jump rings. • Add purchased necklace.

Hanging Vintage Photo with Lace

MATERIALS: 2 pieces 4" x 6" glass • Copy of vintage photo • Lace • Ribbon • 2 large Copper jump rings • Scissors • Bone folder • Solder supplies (solder, iron, flux, ¹/2" Copper tape, Copper Patina)

INSTRUCTIONS: Place vintage photo and lace between two piece of cut glass. • Wrap the edge with Copper tape. Apply a small amount of flux to the top corner of the frame, about ¹/4" away from the edge. Flux the jump ring. Solder jump ring onto the frame. Repeat this step on the other corner of the frame. Clean solder and apply Copper Patina. Thread ribbon through the two jump rings. Tie a bow.

Lace Frame

MATERIALS: 2 pieces 3" x 5" cut glass • Lace • Ball chain • Scissors • Bone folder • Solder supplies (solder, iron, flux, flux remover, ¹/2" Copper tape)

INSTRUCTIONS: Cut lace to fit between the pieces of glass. • Wrap the edges of the glass with Copper tape. • Attach each end of the ball chain on top of the frame with ³/4" long pieces of Copper tape. Flux and solder over the entire frame and the connecting ball chain. Clean with flux remover.

Pressed Flower Pendants

MATERIALS: Pressed flowers • Cut glass shapes • Jump ring • Purchased necklace chain • Scissors • Bone folder • Solder supplies (solder, iron, flux, flux remover, Copper tape)

INSTRUCTIONS: Place dried flower between 2 pieces of cut glass. Wrap the edges with Copper tape. • Flux and solder over Copper tape. Add flux to jump ring and solder onto the top of the pendent. • Clean with flux remover. • Add necklace chain.

1. Paint wood with pigment ink.

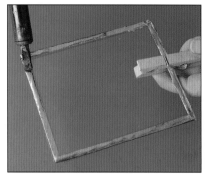

2. Solder edge of glass.

3. Mount photo on wood.

4. Apply Red Liner tape.

5. Adhere glass to wood.

Art Frames
by Carrie Edelmann-Avery

Soldering around the frame gives a beautiful edge to the photo and draws your eye into the picture. Beaded dangles add a bit of sparkle and movement to this practical and pretty artwork.

Cleo Frame

MATERIALS: Balsa wood • 4" x 5" cut glass • Photo • *Making Memories* metal letters • 1/8" eyelets • Jump rings • Eye pins • Beads • Chain • *ColorBox* pigment ink pads • Pliers (needle-nose, chain-nose) • *American Tag* Home Pro Tool • Wire cutters • Scissors • Solder supplies (solder, iron, flux, Copper tape, 1/8" double-sided heat-resistant tape) • *JudiKins* Diamond Glaze • Glue stick

INSTRUCTIONS: Rub pigment ink directly onto balsa wood. Let dry completely. • Wrap edges of glass with Copper tape. Flux and solder. Clean soldered glass. • Glue photo to balsa wood. Apply heat-resistant tape around the edges of the back side of the glass. • Remove backing and adhere on top of photo. Adhere metal letters to wood using Diamond Glaze. • Using Home Pro Tool, punch holes through wood. You will need two holes at the top of the frame to hang the chain and three holes at the bottom of the frame for beaded dangles. Set eyelets. • Make beaded dangles from eye pins and add a charm at the end (See page 9). • Add a chain to the top of the frame using jump rings.

1. Apply Red Liner tape to the glass.

2. Burnish copper tape to edge of glass.

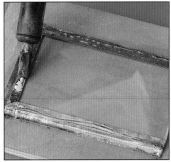

3. Solder over tape.

4. Clean the glass.

Copper and Wood Frame

Why spend hours searching antique shops and paying their rates when you can make your own vintage copper frames?

The photos slide out for quick changes so this is a good gift idea.

The vintage copper provides a proper setting for any old photograph, but it is also lovely when combined with wedding photos.

Vintage Copper Frame

MATERIALS: 2³/4" x 4" cut glass • Balsa wood • Photo • Eyelets • Eye pins • Watch faces • Beads • Jump rings • Chain • *ColorBox* pigment ink pads • *American Tag* Home Pro Tool • Bone folder • Solder supplies (solder, iron, flux, ¹/2" Copper tape, Copper patina, ¹/4" heat-resistant double-sided tape) • E6000

INSTRUCTIONS: Rub pigment ink pads directly onto balsa wood. Let dry completely. • Apply ¹/4" heat-resistant tape around three of the edges of the glass. This will allow you to change pictures in the frame by simply sliding them in and out. Glue the glass to the wood. • Apply Copper tape around the three taped sides of glass. Using a bone folder, burnish the tape well against the glass and onto the wood. Apply flux and solder over the Copper tape. Apply Copper solder patina. Clean and polish the piece. Punch holes and set eyelets using the Home Pro Tool. • Add beaded dangles with eye pins (See page 9). • Punch holes through vintage watch faces and attach to the end of the eye pin. • Add a chain to the top of the frame with jump rings.

Solder on Canvas

by Erin Edelmann

Canvas isn't just for paint. You can solder on it too! Give your canvas art a new dimension with this interesting texture.

Cowgirl Canvas

MATERIALS: *Tara* Canvas • *Paper Loft* decorative paper • *Golden* Fluid Acrylics (Raw Umber, Yellow Ochre) • Sponge • Coffee cup • *Triangle Coatings* (Sophisticated Finishes Blackened Bronze Metal paint; Blue Patina Solution) • Solder supplies (solder, iron, flux, 3/8" Copper tape, Black patina) • Glue stick.

INSTRUCTIONS: Glue western-themed paper to canvas. Dip sponge into Raw Umber and Yellow Ochre fluid acrylic paint. Drag the edge of the sponge from the edge of the canvas towards the middle with light pressure. Dip bottom of an old coffee cup into Blackened Bronze Metal Paint and stamp it all over the paper. While metal paint is still wet, sponge on Blue patina solution over the paint. • Lay down 3/8" metal tape in the shape of the letters to spell "cowgirl". Flux and solder on top of Copper tape. Apply Black patina to solder.

Under the Sea Canvas

MATERIALS: *Design Originals* #0605 Deep Sea paper • *Ampersand* Flat Clayboard • *Triangle Coatings* (Sophisticated Finishes Blackened Bronze metal paint; Blue Patina Solution) • Coffee cup • Sea sponge • Solder supplies (solder, iron, flux, 3/8" Copper tape, Copper patina) • Glue stick

INSTRUCTIONS: Adhere decorative paper to clayboard with glue stick. Sponge Blackened Bronze metal paint directly to the paper. Apply the same paint to the bottom of a coffee cup and stamp randomly around the paper. While the paint is still wet, apply Blue patina solution. • Place Copper tape in a straight line across the clayboard. Flux and solder over the Copper tape. Apply Copper solder patina.

Frida Canvas

MATERIALS: *Design Originals* #0547 Dictionary paper • Canvas • *Bearing Beads* Frida Kahlo image • *Making Memories* alphabet stamps • *Golden* Fluid Acrylics paint (Transparent Red Iron Oxide, Hansa Yellow Medium, Raw Umber) • Walnut Ink • Sponge • *Tsukineko* Staz-On ink • *Triangle Coatings* (Sophisticated Finishes Blackened Bronze Metallic paint; Patina Blue Antiquing Solution) • Solder supplies (solder, iron, 3/8" Silvered Copper tape, Copper and Black patina) • PVA glue

INSTRUCTIONS: Adhere printed paper to canvas with PVA glue. Stamp words using permanent ink directly onto printed paper. • Paint around the top and edges of the picture with walnut ink. • Mix the following Fluid Acrylic colors: Transparent Red Iron Oxide, Hansa Yellow Medium, and Raw Umber. Using a sponge, drag the paint from the edge of the canvas towards the inner picture. Let dry. • Sponge on Blackened Bronze metallic surfacer in selective areas. While it is still wet, sponge on the Patina Blue right on top. The patina will continue to intensify as it dries. • Place 3/8" Silvered Copper tape directly onto the canvas. Anchor ends of the tape around the back side of the canvas frame. Solder on metal tape and patina solder using Copper, then Black patina.

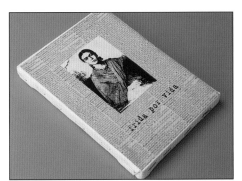

1. Adhere paper. Stamp words.

2. Apply walnut ink.

3. Add paint to edges.

4. Sponge surface with Patina Blue.

5. Apply copper tape.

6. Solder over copper tape.

Solder on Boxes

Soldering can be done on a variety of different surfaces, as long as they are fairly heat resistant. Mica, wood, paper mache, gourds, and other natural materials make a great surface for decorative soldering.

On these projects, the soldering adds sparkle and beauty to the piece. Everyone loves trinket boxes. These decorative items are lovely to own and even more special to give as gifts. The possibilities are only limited by your imagination.

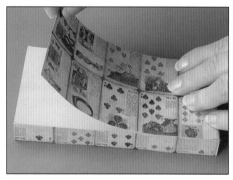

1. Cover box with paper.

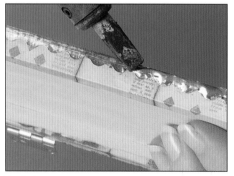

2. Solder over scalloped tape.

3. Apply patina.

Preserve delicate pressed flowers to dress up your bedroom table all year around, or go for the more playful games box. The passionate red heart box is fabulous for any occasion, especially anniversaries.

Turn your creativity loose with these unique ideas.

Game Box
by Laura Dehart

MATERIALS: *Design Originals* #0597 Fortune Cards paper • Wooden box • Scalloped Copper tape • Small glass rectangle • *7gypsies* Game Tile paper • Dice • Solder supplies (solder, iron, flux, 1/4" Copper tape, Copper patina) • *JudiKins* Diamond Glaze • PVA glue

INSTRUCTIONS: Cover the wooden box with decorative paper using PVA glue. Apply scalloped Copper tape to covered box, butting the straight edge against the edge of the box. • Slightly overlap the tape for better adhesion. Flux and solder over the Copper tape. Apply Copper solder patina. • Cut out game letters to spell "Play" and adhere over decorative paper. • Wrap the edges of the smaller glass piece with Copper tape. Flux, solder, and patina. • Adhere words and glass piece to the top of the box using Diamond Glaze. Adhere dice to the bottom of the box with Diamond Glaze.

Heart Box
by Linda Rael

MATERIALS: Copper sheet • Ceramic box • Flower punch • *Jacquard* (Pinata ink, Extender) • Paintbrush • Solder supplies (solder, iron, flux, Copper tape) • E6000

INSTRUCTIONS: Clean ceramic box and add Copper tape on the bottom and the rim. Punch flower shape from Copper sheet. • Flux and solder over Copper tape and the flower. • Paint the box with Pinata inks, adding a few drop of extender to the surface for texture. Let dry. • Glue the flower to lid.

Les Fleurs
by Linda Rael

MATERIALS: Clip art • Dried flowers • Microscope slide glass • Copper tape • Paper mache box • Acrylic paint • *Hero Arts* alphabet stamps • *ColorBox* permanent ink • Solder supplies (solder, iron, flux, 1/4" Copper tape) • *JudiKins* Diamond Glaze

INSTRUCTIONS: Layer clip art and dried flowers on the back of the microscope slide. Adhere with Diamond Glaze. • Wrap slide with Copper tape. Apply Copper tape around the box. Flux and solder over the Copper tape. • Paint the box with acrylic paint. Stamp letters directly onto the box with permanent ink. Let dry. • Adhere glass slide to the lid of the box with Diamond Glaze.

Boxes and Books

If you can't find a box you want to decorate, or you just want to follow your own artistic muse, you can design and construct your own original box held together with soldering. As you can see, the materials available cross a range from mounts to tin. I hope you enjoy exploring the possibilities of this idea.

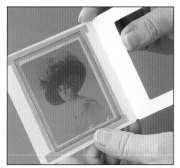

1. Adhere the transparency to the mount.

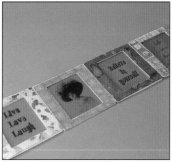

2. Line up mounts.

3. Apply copper tape.

4. Form into a box.

5. Sandwich the transparency between 2 sheets of Mica Tile.

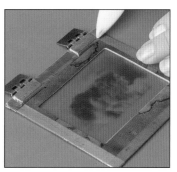

6. Burnish copper tape over the hinges.

7. Add patina.

Metal Muerto Box
by Laura Dehart

MATERIALS: *AMACO* aluminum sheets (6 each medium & heavy weight 3¹/2" x 4") • Rubber stamps (*Stamp Antonio* Muertos; *Uptown* Shrine of the Divine) • *Tsukineko* Staz-On ink pad • Stylus tool or pen • *Making Memories* hinges • Epoxy glue • Sharp scissors • Solder supplies (solder, iron, flux, ¹/2" Copper tape, Black patina)

INSTRUCTIONS: Stamp the Shrine with permanent ink on medium weight aluminum sheet. Using stylus tool or ball point pen, trace over the sides of shrine. Repeat this step on 5 of the 6 medium weight sheets. Stamp skeleton (muertos) image with permanent ink in the center of each of the embossed metal sheets. Again, trace over the lines of stamped image to leave surface embossed. • Lay four of the embossed metal sheets side by side, leaving a ¹/8" space between them. Lay the heavy weight aluminum sheets, cut to same size, over each of the four pieces. Adhere each of the panels together with the 3¹/2" Copper tape. Form into box shape. Adhere plain aluminum panel to bottom of box with Copper tape. Flux, solder and patina over the Copper tape. Glue hinges to the last panel and to one of the sides of the box.

Slide Mount Box
by Laura Dehart

MATERIALS: *Design Originals* (#0622 Beauties Transparency; Mounts: #0980 Water Marks, #0983 Tapes) • *USArtQuest* Mica Tiles • *Making Memories* hinges • Scissors • Solder supplies (solder, iron, flux, ¹/2" Copper tape, Black patina) • Heat-resistant double-sided tape)

INSTRUCTIONS: Cut out transparency images to fit inside mounts. Adhere the transparencies with heat-resistant double-sided tape to the inside of mount. Lay four mounts side by side. Apply ¹/2" Copper tape, leaving a ¹/8" gap in between. Form the mounts into a box and tape the final joints. • For the top and bottom pieces, sandwich the transparencies between two sheets of mica for stability. With Copper tape, adhere the bottom mount to box. The top slide mount will be joined to the box with hinges that will be adhered with Copper tape. Flux and solder over all of the Copper tape. Apply Black solder patina.

Copper Cat Book
by Linda Rael

MATERIALS: 2 Copper 2" x 2" sheets • Stylus tool or pen • Brown waxed linen thread • Iridescent E-beads • Charms • 2" x 2" papers • Awl • Solder supplies (solder, iron, flux, ¹/2" Copper tape)

INSTRUCTIONS: Emboss Copper sheets with stylus as desired. • Add Copper tape to front and back. Flux and solder. • Punch 3 holes in each Copper sheet for binding. • Punch matching holes in the papers for the inside of the book. • Layer book cover, papers, and back cover. Use waxed linen thread to bind the book together. Add beads and charms to the linen thread as desired.

'Scrimshaw' Jewelry

by Beckah Krahula

Now you can make beautiful faux scrimshaw jewelry using clay and rubber stamps. This technique works best when you choose deeply etched stamps with simple, clear lines. Soldering makes the outer edge of the piece smooth and gives the piece the professional look of real jewelry. These soldered scrimshaw pendants are made from a faux bone polymer clay mixture, but many of the other faux mixtures would work as well.

Faux Bone Scrimshaw Soldered Jewelry

MATERIALS: *Polyform (Premo* clay: 2 oz. block White, 2 oz. block Ecru, two 2 oz. blocks Translucent; Liquid Sculpey) • *Bearing Beads* rubber stamps • Jewelry chain • Jump rings • Brayer • Pasta machine • Parchment paper • Large plain White index card • Clay blade • Craft knife • *Golden* Burnt Umber acrylic paint • *Houston Art* Mixed Media Water based Sealer (gloss or satin) • Q-tips • Needle-nose pliers • Wooden clothespins • Jump Rings • Large bristle brush • Awl • Sanding Discs • Scrap Paper • Scissors • Gin (or water) in a spray bottle • Solder supplies (Solder, Iron, Flux, Jig, 1/4" Copper tape)

INSTRUCTIONS: Choose stamps that are deeply etched line drawings. • With the pasta machine set on #1, separately condition equal parts White and Ecru. Set aside on parchment paper. • Condition 2 bricks of Translucent clay. Cut into 2 equal size pieces.

• Stack the pieces of polymer clay in layers in this order: White, Translucent, Ecru, Translucent. To prevent trapping air bubbles between the layers, hold the piece of clay that is being laid down on the stack by both ends and bow the clay. Lay the center of the bowed clay down on the clay it is being layered onto. Guide down one end, followed by the other end. Run over the layered clay a couple times with a brayer. Press down on the brayer lightly so the clay will stick together, but not hard enough to thin out the clay.

• Cut in half and stack the one half on top of the other. Cut a 2" wedge from the stacked clay. Stack on top of the left-over clay and cut the bottom to match the two-inch piece on top. Set aside the stacked left-over clay and take the 2" wedge to the pasta machine.

• While holding one hand over the clay, roll the clay through the pasta machine on the widest setting. Look at the blend of clays. Fold the clay with the most interesting blend on the outside and run through the machine again. Repeat and stop when the color blend is what you want. Be careful not to overblend.

Use clay in the thickness that it came out of the pasta machine.
• Cut the clay in half and stack it on itself, with the best sides facing out. The 2 layers should be 1/4"- 3/8" in total thickness. Press slightly to get the layers to stick together. In colder weather, add a thin layer of Liquid Sculpey between the layers. Lightly spray the clay with gin (or water) and press the image stamps into the clay about 1" apart. Use firm and heavy pressure, as you want a deeply etched image to be pressed into the clay. Pick a structure stamp and place over an embossed image on the clay. Press the edges down and remove the stamp. The stamp leaves a ditch around the image. Cut the ditch away, then set aside.

• Continue until you have made enough beads for a 7 1/2" bracelet. Make sure your edges are smoothed. Place the beads on a plain White index card. Cure for 30 minutes at 265°. Remove from the oven and let cool. • Sand edges if necessary.

• Brush Burnt Umber paint on all of the beads. Make sure the stamped indentations are filled with paint and that the top surface has paint on it as well. Paint the sides and back. Let dry. This stains and patinas the clay.

• Use wet 400-grit sandpaper to lightly wet sand off most of the paint on the top surface leaving paint in the stamped impressions in the clay. If the image is in danger of being lost from sanding and there is still paint to be removed, use an awl or toothpick to remove the paint. This is very helpful in small areas such as eyes. • Wrap Copper tape around all edges, and burnish.

• Put the pendants in the freezer for about 5 minutes. Soldering is best done in an assembly line fashion so that pieces get a chance to cool. Use the clothespin to hold the pendant if need be. Flux the top edge of the pendant. Open the clothespin wide when removing pendant to solder the next edge so that you do not pull off the Copper tape. Solder all 4 edges. • Place jump ring on top. Wash. Patina if desired.

Solder Accents

by Linda Rael

Solder accents can be applied to many materials. These interesting folk art pieces use solder to create details on gourd figures. The Senorita gourd uses solder to make the layers in the skirt. The long-neck goose has a sparkling soldered beak and solder trim wings. Turn a gourd into a southwest style bowl with soldered lines and metal cut-outs.

Bird
MATERIALS: Gourd • Scalloped Copper tape • Wooden base and ball • Dowel • Feathers • Beads • Twigs • Black waxed linen thread• Scrap of leather • *Golden* Fluid Acrylic (Quinacridone Gold, Chromium Oxide Green) • Sandpaper • *Houston Art* Mona Lisa water-based sealer • Walnut ink • Drill • Solder supplies (solder, iron, flux, 1/4" Copper tape) • Glue
INSTRUCTIONS: Clean and sand gourd. • Apply Copper tape for wings, beak, and eyes. Flux and solder on top of tape. • Paint gourd with Quinacridone Gold and Chromium Oxide Green Fluid Acrylics. • Lightly sand painted areas. • Paint walnut ink over the entire surface. • Seal with water-based sealer. • Paint wooden ball and base. Drill a hole in the bottom of the bird and glue the base, dowel and bird together. • Glue leather around twigs and feathers. Wrap leather with waxed linen thread. Add beads and feathers. Tie embellishment around the bird's neck.

Sun and Stars Gourd
MATERIALS: Gourd • Fibers • Beads • Craft punches • Walnut ink • Acrylic paint • Spray glitter • Drill • Solder supplies (solder, 1/2" Copper tape) • Copper embossing metal • E6000 adhesive
INSTRUCTIONS: Cut the top off the gourd. Sand both the inside and outside of gourd. • Apply Copper tape to gourd. Punch out star and sun shapes from the Copper embossing metal. Melt solder onto the punched shapes. • Paint inside of the gourd with acrylic paint, walnut ink, and spray glitter. • Paint outside of the gourd with acrylic paint and walnut ink. If gourd bottom is not flat, glue a bead or gourd piece to make it level. • Drill hole on front of gourd and add fibers and beads. • Glue Copper shapes onto the surface of gourd.

Senorita
MATERIALS: Bottle gourd • Scalloped Copper tape • 3 Copper beads • Hair yarn • Doily • Stick • Acrylic paint • Assorted rubber stamp images • *Houston Art* Water based Sealer • Sandpaper • Solder supplies (solder, iron, 1/4" Copper tape) • E6000 adhesive
INSTRUCTIONS: Clean and sand gourd. • Run Copper tape around bulb part of gourd for the skirt. Melt solder onto tape and onto Copper beads (which will be used for eyes and nose). • Paint with acrylic paints, stamp designs. Seal with water based sealer. Glue yarn for hair. Add stick for arms and doily for shawl. Glue on eyes and nose.

Winged Pendants

*by Ramona Dolan Ashman
and Tom Ashman*

Make a pendant for the angel in your life or express your free spirit with this butterfly. The copper plate makes the project both shiny and sturdy while the transparency film creates a lovely gossamer wing effect. What a lovely way to use glass slides!

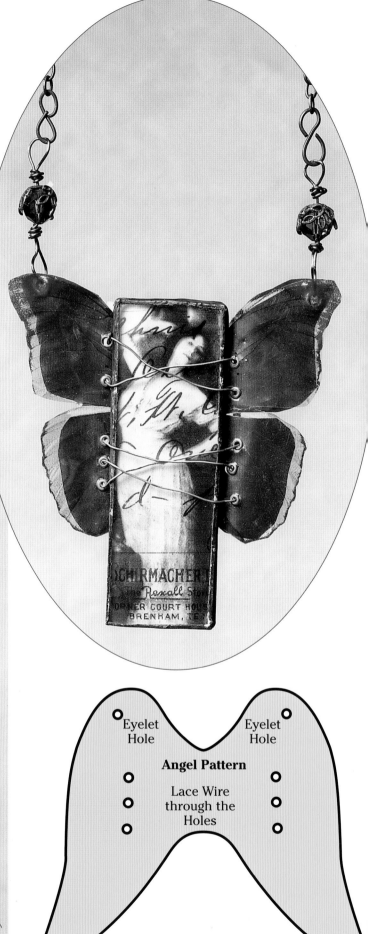

Angel Pattern

Eyelet Hole

Eyelet Hole

Lace Wire through the Holes